The Mature Student's

Guide to Tackling a

Post-Secondary Education

Going back to school as an adult

Elizabeth Harriman

ISBN: **978-1-4357-1623-0**

Dedication

This book is dedicated to my wonderful, supportive family,
without whom my own education would not have been possible.
It is to their credit that this book was possible.

Thank you for bearing with me.

I owe you everything.

Contents

Introduction

*Get over the idea that only children should spend
their time in study.
Be a student so long as you still have something to learn,
and this will mean all your life.*
~Henry L. Doherty

So, you want to go back to school. (Doesn't every great self-help book start out that way?) You are making the right decision. And believe me, I've been a mature student twice now, and I know first hand the joy and benefit a post-secondary education brings.

There are however, a lot of things to consider, and some changes you can make that will make your life a lot easier as you work your way towards graduation. It took my family and me years to figure it all out and muddle our way through, but it can be done. Thousands of people do it every day, and so can you. Don't let yourself believe that it's your decision alone though. If you are married, have a partner, have children, work full or part-time, you need to make the decision as a family as it will impact everyone's lives. It really does take everyone working together to make it happen.

The first time I went back to school as a mature student, I was 25, divorced and living on my own in a new city with a four-year old. I had quit my job, moved eight hundred miles and enrolled in classes in a community college. It was one of the most exciting times of my life, and I simply couldn't wait to dig in and get going. Everything was new and fresh. I chose a small campus, the program I was interested in, had all my finances, payment of tuition and fees sorted out, and was jumping in with both feet. Granted it was easier then. I was able to attend classes on a full-time basis and my 2-year program took exactly what it should have: 2 years. I didn't have to go to work, enroll only in classes that were offered in the evening, arrange to leave work early on certain days, or try to arrange my vacation schedule around my exam schedule.

The second time I became a mature student I was 34, married again, now with two children, 14 and 4, working full time and just as excited as the first time. I applied and was accepted to Bock University as a part-time student. This time I had a different goal in mind, different interests and a different path already chosen to follow. I also had different obstacles to overcome and I had completely underestimated what it would take to make everything work with an already overloaded plate to contend with. I hadn't yet realized what a balancing act this was going to be.

This time, I had to keep my full-time job and juggle all of my responsibilities at once. I was limited to courses offered at night. Thanks to a very understanding workplace, they allowed me to tweak my hours a bit so that I could make it to late afternoon classes, which expanded my course choices. Family, work and school all have to be given attention, and must be considered. Where do you find the time it all takes in a 24-hour day? Well, I still haven't figured that out, but the chapters that I cover in this book will definitely ease the strain and lead you in the right direction. With a bit of careful planning and forethought, the path to graduation can be much simpler than you think.

This book will help you understand the schools and how to find the information you need. I'll talk about making sure that everyone in the family is on board and how your success as a student relies on the members of your house working as a team. If you are single, this isn't as much of an issue and you've got less to worry about and fewer factors to consider. We'll look at family and vacation time as well as study time and see how to get them all lined up to keep you more organized and stress-free. Time management is big part of getting your education without neglecting everything else in your life, especially if your plate is as full as mine. Without it, it's easy to lose track, lose focus, and lose your way.

A post-secondary education can open up many doors for you. Better and higher paying positions will become available, promotions, or even a brand new career. Maybe you are like me – in an ok job, with ok money, but you know there's something better out there just waiting for you. So what's standing in your way? An education.

It's a fact that people who have post-secondary educations get better jobs and earn more money. In today's market, a high school diploma just isn't going to get you very far unless your dream job is flipping burgers or answering phones for the person sitting behind the big mahogany desk who does have that college or university diploma hanging on the wall behind them. I'd prefer to be the person behind the desk.

According to the 2004-2005 Ontario University Graduate

Survey, two years after graduation the average salary for a person with an undergraduate degree was $43,578. According to the same people, the Council of Ontario's Universities (www.cou.on.ca), the holder of a bachelor's degree will earn $488,500 more over their lifetime than someone holding only a high school diploma. You can see that there is a significant difference. I look at it as motivation.

If you are not looking to advance your career but rather want to take courses for personal interest, the ideas presented in this book can help you as well. Post-secondary institutions have a large population of mature students, some more mature than others. I have met some students who are past retirement, and have gone back to school for their own enjoyment. It's wonderful to meet these people and benefit from their life experience. They are all enjoying their experience in school and so should you. There's nothing better than expanding your mind, learning new things and encountering new ideas and concepts. It's a win-win situation no matter how you look at it or from which direction you approach it.

If you are seriously thinking about becoming a student again, you've come to the right place. Now, let's get you started!

One

Computers and Getting Connected

*The great thing about a computer notebook is
that no matter how much you stuff into it,
it doesn't get bigger or heavier.
~ Bill Gates*

If you are not computer literate, you really need to get that way. Get your children to teach you, hire the kid down the street, take some classes - do something, but get good and comfortable with your computer and the internet. Most community colleges offer some basic beginner courses on operating computers, as well as using some of the more common software programs. There are also some great how-to books available that can help you get started.

One of the most useful tools you'll have in your arsenal is a good laptop with a reliable battery, an internet connection and a word processing software package. Taking notes by hand is great, but taking notes on a laptop is much easier and quicker. Unless you can use shorthand or write at lightning speed, your notes will be clearer, neater, and you'll be able to record a lot more than if you are trying to capture important points from your lecture by hand. Some professors lecture at about the same speed as an auctioneer sells antiques! Clear, concise notes are an important part of your success as a student, so why not make it as easy as possible? Laptops come in all sizes, and even in various colors. Some are smaller and lighter than others, but it seems that the smaller, more compact models unfortunately come with a heftier price tag. Go figure. Smaller = more expensive. Less bulk yet a bulkier price tag.

Buying a laptop, or any computer for that matter, can be a trying experience, especially if you don't have a solid understanding of things like RAM, gigabytes, processor speeds, hard drives, mother boards, DVD versus CD writers, burners, etc. It's enough to make your own hard drive spin. That's where the salesperson comes in handy. Make a list of what you want to be able to do with your computer. Don't limit yourself to word processing. If you want to be able to watch movies on your computer make sure you include that. If you want to burn CDs or DVDs, include that too. If you want to be able to work with graphics and pictures, write that down as well. These people get paid to know their stuff, so take advantage of it. They'll be able to answer your questions and provide you with the information you'll need to make an educated purchase.

There are a lot of places where you can compare laptops and do a little research before you hit the stores. Magazines dedicated to computers are a good place to start or you can perform an online search using words such as "computer", "comparison" or any other word you think may apply. If you are interested in buying a Macintosh product, you may have to include the words "Macintosh" or "Apple" in your search.

Along with the computer itself, make sure you look into a warranty. There are different warranty plans available and most reputable stores will offer, and usually recommend buying one. I recommend getting one as well. A few years ago I had purchased a brand new laptop and before it was a year old, the screen went blank. I couldn't see a thing even though I could hear things whirring and going on inside. The entire cost of repairs and shipping was included and covered by the warranty. If you don't have that warranty, your brand new computer may end up being useless should anything go wrong and you'll incur the extra cost of having it repaired, including parts, labour and shipping if necessary

A reliable battery is important because it's a pain to have to switch from your laptop to paper and pen half way through your three-hour lecture. You don't generally have a choice of batteries, but you can buy upgraded batteries at an additional cost. Electrical outlets can be hard to come by in lecture halls, and you'll see a lot of the laptop-toting students congregating near the outlets with a web of power cords around their feet. Remember that back when most of these buildings were being built, computers simply didn't exist so there was no need for students to need electrical outlets. These days however, more and more students are choosing to use them in lecture. In my experience an Apple laptop is the way to go. I've had both pc and Apple products under my arm and in my bag at school, and the Apple battery outperforms the pc and wins by a landslide. When my pc laptop was brand new the battery would not get me through a 3-hour lecture without being plugged in. This past winter I bought a used, older model Apple laptop from Ebay and packed it into my bag along with the power cord fully expecting to be plugged in by mid-evening. To my surprise, by the end of class the battery was only down to half capacity. There was not once when I needed to plug that sucker in. (Ok. So that's not completely true. I forgot to charge the battery one night and left the next day with a completely drained battery. I ended up having another student email me their notes from that lecture because it was so much easier than trying to write by hand.)

There have been several times during a lecture when the professor was addressing one subject or another, and I was able to perform a search for more information from right there in my chair. During one French class, I realized that I needed to get my hands on a particular book. I figured that most of the other students were likely thinking the same thing. Because my trusty Apple has wireless capabilities, I logged onto the school library, searched for and located the book I needed, and placed a hold on it before anyone else got their grubby little hands on it. All done without leaving my seat and the whole process took about three minutes. Most post-secondary institutions have wireless internet on most, if not all school property these days, and you'll see students taking full advantage of it. Besides, during a particularly boring lecture, you can always check your email or chat with a friend using instant messaging.

Not that I've ever done that.

Fine. I admit it. I've done it.

Wireless capability is a true miracle. If you are going to purchase a new laptop, ask the sales people at the store if it does indeed come with wireless capabilities. Most do these days, but it never hurts to make sure. Apple products are generally more expensive than pc's, but in my humble opinion, you get what you pay for.

You'll also need a wireless router for use at home if you want to have the freedom of a wireless connection, and be able to plunk yourself down anywhere away from those ethernet cords. These can cost anywhere from 70 to 200 dollars depending on what you want to buy and how many computers in your home you want to access it. A wireless router will allow you to connect to the internet from your laptop through the router, without having that darned cable dragging behind you as you move around the house. You can get a very good wireless router in the 70 – 80 dollar range. Your service provider should be able to help you set this up over the phone by calling their technical help people. Some manufacturers also have technical help lines if you have trouble installing or operating your modem. If that seems like too much trouble, don't worry. You can still plug a wireless laptop into your ethernet cable the same way a desktop model gets plugged in. And voila! Internet at your fingertips.

The internet is a great resource for fact finding, research and a host of other things. There are online dictionaries, thesauruses, conversion functions for anything you can think of, language translation, and the list goes on and on and on. A lot of research for projects, assignments and essays can be done partially online, so having access to the internet is really a valuable tool.

In my first year I decided to take the introductory French course that was being offered. I thought this would be a pretty easy course, since I'm bilingual to begin with. It was all fine and dandy until we started verb conjugation and I realized that after 20 years out of school, my verb conjugating abilities really left something to be desired. I hopped on the internet and searched for practice lessons to help me relearn what I'd forgotten and get me back into shape. I found a few websites that were really good and helped tremendously. By spending a few hours online practicing and relearning what I'd forgotten my mark went up considerably. There are fantastic websites for just about anything you want to know. You just have to look for them!

Most computers will have a calendar program installed, which makes keeping track of classes and their locations, essay due dates and assignments much easier. I highly recommend taking advantage of this as workload and due dates can sometimes become a little overwhelming. There's nothing worse than thinking you have another week to prepare that 2500 word essay, only to discover at the last minute that it's due tomorrow! Depending on which program you decide on, you'll find lots of little ways to help keep yourself on track. You can set reminders which will pop up on the screen, you can flag items to be followed up on, as well as set start and end dates for projects by following an agenda that you set up yourself.

You'll also need a good word processing program for the

volumes of notes and essays you'll be writing, and the standard seems to be Microsoft Word, which comes as part of the suite bundled with a few other programs. Microsoft also has a Macintosh version, so if you choose to go with an Apple, you are good to go. One of the nicest little tools that Microsoft has in its Word program is the ability to keep track of reference materials that you use for your essays. By entering the information once, the reference information you enter is stored, and when it comes time to create your list of works cited at the end of your paper, it's all there ready and waiting for you. Microsoft suites come packaged in several versions. Some are more expensive offering more in the bundled suite, and some a less expensive but offer fewer programs If you already have student card, you can likely purchase the teacher/student version at a reduced cost. When I bought mine however, I was never asked to produce anything stating that I was either a teacher or a student.

There are other word processing programs available that work nicely. As some professors prefer to have essays emailed to them instead of having piles of paper to lug around, it would be worth your while to find out what the most commonly acceptable program or file format is at your school before you purchase it. Once that little box containing the software has been opened, it's sometimes almost impossible to return it! Better to be safe than sorry, and get the information first before shelling out a couple of hundred bucks for it.

If a new laptop is out of your price range, you can buy a used one. When I bought my Apple from Ebay, I paid about $400 US for a refurbished model that was about four years old at the time. There was an extra cost to have the operating system upgraded to a more current version, and another extra cost to have the wireless modem installed. Both extra expenses were well worth the money I paid, but certainly were not necessary. The total cost including shipping was about $700 US. Good used systems are available through used computer stores, newspaper classifieds, and of course, Ebay. I'm sure you can find them in a lot of other places too. Again, you just have to look for them.

Stores carrying new models usually have "open-box" deals, which could include models that have been on display or refurbished systems. These are usually available at lower costs, although they might have a scratch here and there. Think of it as the "dent and scratch" section of the store. There are some really good deals out there just waiting for you. Keep your eyes open for sales as well. Don't be so quick to toss out the weekly delivery of flyers before you've had a chance to flip through the electronics section. Sometimes stores offer great sales, and occasionally bundle software with your computer purchase, although this is more likely with the purchase of a new model rather than an open box model.

Another option is a payment plan, however there are usually fairly high interest rates associated with in-store credit options. If you have a low interest line of credit, that might be the most economical way to finance your purchase.

If a used laptop isn't in your budget either, don't fret. With practice, your note taking skills will improve and you can, of course, get by without one. After all, people have done it for centuries!

Before I started bringing a laptop with me to class, I had a heck of time keeping up and my notes were a disaster with words scratched out and arrows pointing here, there and everywhere. Over time, I developed my own version of a shorthand system, which consisted of abbreviations and symbols to cut down on both the amount of words I needed to write as well as the time it took me to write them. If you are going to go with the "paper and pen" method instead of a laptop, make sure that you have access to one, either through a friend, your local library or a desktop model at home. You will need to use one for essays and assignments that need to be handed in. You will also need to access the internet to find information on schools, to access the required forms, browse the schools' online calendars, course selection and registration as well as get pertinent information you'll need for your classes. These topics will all be covered in later chapters.

One last word about computers - make sure that you purchase a good antivirus program. There is probably nothing more frustrating than losing all of your notes, essays, contacts, calendar items etc. because some moron decided to send you another Viagra spam-mail which took your hard drive and turned it into a fatally afflicted coma patient, leaving you with the blue screen of death. (This, by the way, doesn't happen on Apples, as far as I know. At least, I've never heard of it.)

One more last word about computers, and I swear this is the last one. One of the best ways to decide which computer, software and antivirus packages to buy is to ask people you know what they recommend. Couple this strategy with doing some consumer sales investigations and you are likely to get the perfect system for you. Sales people, although a wealth of information may be hesitant to give you the cons as well as the pros, and are likely to try to oversell the product, by telling you that you need more than you actually do. People you know personally are more likely to tell you the truth about their experiences with certain products, what they liked, what they disliked, what was a lemon, what worked like a charm, and what just plain didn't work. Tap into this hidden resource. If people have had a bad experience with something, trust me. They'll want to tell you about it.

Two

Choosing a Program

Good schools, like good societies and good families,
celebrate and cherish diversity.
~ Deborah Meier

One of the first things you'll want to consider while planning your education is what subject you'd like to study. This will have a direct impact on what school you choose to apply to. Since not every school offers every program, you'll likely have to do a bit of poking around to find what you are looking for.

When I applied to Brock University, I knew exactly what I wanted to study and what my intent was. I had a plan in place, and thought I knew exactly how to get from the beginning of my studies to the end. After my first year was completed however, I changed paths completely.

My original plan was to follow a particular program, leading to teacher's college and then on to a teaching career. I had really given no thought to teachable subjects or minors. The first two classes I took were Introduction to Psychology (which is still one of the most interesting classes I've taken so far) and the first year introductory French course. The next course I planned on taking was Sociology, which is a required course as well as a pre-requisite to other courses (I'll explain that later). As it turns out, the first year Sociology course was very rarely offered at a time when I could take it. As a full-time employee working straight days, I was only able to take evening classes. This put a definite hitch in my plans. I needed to take Sociology because it was a pre-requisite for a lot of the other courses I needed to take. Without that course I was at a standstill and I needed to re-evaluate my plan.

After doing a little research, I wondered if I could take it at another university on a Letter of Permission (I'll explain this later too). The answer, to my dismay, was no. I didn't have enough Brock credits to qualify to take a course at another institution. You can see how this quickly became a source of much frustration. I was stuck between a rock and a hard place. I needed to take course before I could take other, but I couldn't take the course because of the time it was offered.

When Spring Session rolled around, I wanted to use my time effectively and spend my summer taking another class. By doing this, I crammed a one-year course (September to April) into eight weeks running from late April to mid July. Instead of attending class once per week for 3 hours, I would attend 2 nights per week for four hours each night. I looked at what was being offered that would fit into my plan, and enrolled in an English literature course. This is when my original well-laid plan came to a screeching halt and took a totally different direction.

I took a good look at the course calendar and realized that

French and English courses were regularly offered in the evenings. Not only had I really enjoyed that first English class but after some investigation, I discovered that I could finish with a combined degree in English Literature and French. This meant that I would finish my degree with two teachable subjects instead of just one, or none. To teach senior high school grades in Ontario you need two teachable subjects instead of the one you need to teach lower grades. A combined degree meant simply that I would take an equal number of English Literature courses and French courses, along with the required context credits and electives. It was perfect!

Your decision may also depend on what you are planning to do with your education. Are you thinking of teaching? Perhaps you want to continue on in the same field you are currently working in, but need an education to move up the ladder, so to speak. Your reasons for attending post-secondary will likely play a very big role in deciding what to study, which program to choose, and ultimately what institution to apply to.

What is a program? Quite simply, it's the subject area. In university, each program falls into a category called a faculty. The most common faculties are Business, Humanities, Mathematics and Science, and Social Sciences. Some institutions include additional faculties such as Applied Health Sciences and Education. Others may only offer a few of the above depending on the size of the school, and some may offer more.

Within each faculty, different programs are offered. For example, the Faculty of Mathematics and Science may include

Biological Sciences, Biochemistry, Computer Science, Earth Science or Geography. The Faculty of Humanities may include Language Studies, Literature, Philosophy or Studies in Arts and Culture.

You will eventually have to choose a major or combined major like I did, a major with a minor, or a major with a concentration in a specific area. What does all that mean? A major is a course of studies that is comprised of only one area of study. Let's say Sociology. A combined major I've already explained; it's a degree with two equal subject areas; in my case, English Literature and French. A major with a minor is a main area of study, such as Sociology with a smaller portion of your studies devoted to a secondary and different subject area. So, you could have a major in Sociology with a minor in Geography. A major with a concentration is your main area of study, enabling students to pursue studies within their major or combined major program. For example, you could major in Sociology with a concentration in Criminology or Social Justice and Equity.

So let's look at this in a simpler way. Let's say you want to pursue an undergraduate degree in mixology. You are not likely to find anywhere offering this type of degree, but its fun to imagine anyway. You can pursue a major in mixology, consisting of courses focused on mixing up yummy drinks with a variety of alcohol. You can pursue a combined major in mixology and flower arranging - two separate subject matters split more or less equally in two. Next on the list is a major in mixology and a minor in tree planting. Your course of studies would be mostly mixology with a smaller portion of tree planting courses – two separate subjects. Finally, you could work towards a major in mixology with a concentration, or focus, on vodka-based drinks. I'm sure that simplified explanation makes much more sense.

Although each post-secondary institution may have different policies and regulations, as well as requirements, the concept remains pretty much the same no matter where you go.

Community colleges offer different programs. In Canada, community colleges offers programs that train you in particular field such as graphic arts, early childhood education, medical office administration, advanced police studies and many more. They also offer apprenticeships such as auto-body collision and repair, steamfitter and sheet metal worker.

So where are you going to find all of this information? Each college and university has a website, and all of this information should be available there. Course calendars are like a menu of what is offered. You may be able to get a print copy of the institution's course calendar for a fee, but more and more schools are moving away from this costly practice and only offering their calendar online.

This actually works well for all involved for a number of reasons. There's no cost to you to access the calendar online, and there's no printing, production or shipping costs for the school, nor do you need to order a new calendar each year to keep up to date on revisions, changes, additions or deletions. Hyperlinks are built into the calendar, essentially allowing you to jump from one topic to a related topic and back again, with one or two clicks of the mouse. You can also have more than one window open allowing you to view more than one area of the calendar at a time. With a printed version, you'd be flipping back and forth through the pages and running the terrible risk of numerous paper cuts. This way, you cut down considerably on band-aids.

If you are fortunate, there will be an institution nearby that offers exactly what you are looking for. But what happens if there isn't? If you live in a large urban area, chances are that you'll have no trouble finding what you are looking for. For example, there are seven or eight universities and probably an equal amount of colleges within driving distance from where I live. My choices were wide and varied, and I had the opportunity to really look at what each school offered and make my decision based on personal preference. However, not everyone is as fortunate.

If you live in an area where there are no schools nearby, or that do not offer the program you want to take, you'll need to consider other options. There are a few different things you can consider. First, you can modify your choice according what your local school has to offer. Or, if you are not willing to do that, then you need to investigate other avenues such as distance education.

Three

Distance or Campus Classes?

I like a teacher who gives you something to take home
to think about besides homework.
~ Edith Ann, [Lily Tomlin]

Distance education is a great alternative and comes in a variety of formats. My personal experience and opinion regarding distance education is two-sided.

I wanted to take an extra course while I was attending classes at Brock, but I didn't want to spend a third night per week away from home. I started investigating distance courses offered through other institutions, as Brock does not offer distance courses at all. I thought this option would work well and would fit in perfectly with my already overtaxed schedule.

If this option interests you, keep in mind that not every school offers distance education, while others offer nothing but. The rest fall somewhere in between. To find institutions that offer distance education, you can search the internet for "distance education". It will be helpful to include your country of residence in your search criteria as well. Once you've got a list of institutions, spend some time browsing their online calendars and websites. They will have their faculties listed, along with undergraduate programs and graduate programs. You will also be able to access a list of courses and programs they offer. These lists will outline the courses, the formats they are being offered in and will likely provide you with a list of required reading materials. This is a nice advantage because you can see what you will be reading before you enroll in the course. In fact, this was one of the deciding factors I used when considering which course to enroll in. If you really don't like the material, you can simply move on down the list and pick another course. You will have to investigate whether the textbooks are included in the cost of the course or whether they need to be purchased separately.

I really enjoy the freedom of distance education. You can work at your own pace (within reason) when you have the time, without having to be in class at a specified hour. Nor do you have to worry about classes interfering with work or family commitments, or driving in bad weather. The school that I used for distance education gives you twelve months to complete your course, with the option of applying for a three-month extension if needed. You can do this twice, however there is a fee of approximately $150 dollars for each extension application. Unless you are very committed, you can quickly and easily fall behind in your studies.

In my opinion, an important aspect of the learning experience is missing from this type of studying. While sitting in a classroom or lecture hall, you have the opportunity to ask questions and get immediate answers. You hear questions from classmates which may provoke thoughts and ideas that you otherwise would not have considered. You miss out on spontaneous discussion, which I think is an important part of the learning process. Putting your thoughts into words and hearing the thoughts and ideas of your classmates only adds to the content and richness of your classes.

Some distance classes offer group discussions via the internet, in the form of an online forum. This is similar to bulletin boards where you post messages and other people can see and respond to them. This may be one way to bridge the gap that exists between formal classroom instruction and distance learning, although not all institutions or particular classes will offer this option. Even though the spontaneity is still missing, it is another way for students to share their ideas and communicate. These forums are also set up for a number of traditional classes, allowing the students an extra outlet for discussion.

One professor I had in the past would pose a question at the end of every lecture. The students were invited to think about the question, and post their thoughts on the online forum, where other students could comment or post their own thoughts. This was a very helpful way to continue learning and thinking even after the class was done for the week. It was almost as if the class was continuing, only this time from my own couch.

Distance education, depending on the institution, is offered in a variety of formats. The more traditional print format includes printed books that you are required to read, and are generally included in the cost of the course. The course materials will be mailed to you at home prior to the start date of your course. Any supplementary learning materials will arrive as well, all neatly packaged in your box.

Some institutions offer other formats. These may include internet-based courses. I have yet to take a course in this format but I find the concept interesting, and I'm sure you'll agree, convenient. Lessons and lecture notes may also be available in print on the website. Another format is the video format, where pre-taped or "canned" lectures are sent to you in a video format either on VHS or CD. This way, you can watch the lecture as many times as you need which is a nice touch. I've often wished I could replay my lecture so that I could hear it over again. I'm sure that over the years there has been a ton of things that I've missed for one reason or another.

Each course has a "teacher", and you are welcome to email your questions or thoughts to them or contact them by telephone during their regular office hours. They will inform you of their email address, phone number and office hours. You will never be without a person to discuss the course subject with. Your essays and assignments will also be sent via email to your "teacher" and will be returned to you, again via email, with your mark and any applicable comments, the same way you'd have your work returned to you in a traditional classroom setting.

If you have more questions about a certain institution, contact the Registrar's Office or Student Services at that school. Most schools will have a list of contacts on their website, along with an FAQ (frequently asked questions) section where you'll be able to find answers to most or all of your questions. Remember that the people who work there are getting paid to provide you, the consumer, with timely and complete answers to your questions. Yet another resource available for you to take full advantage of.

A full list of colleges and universities should be listed on the education section of your provincial or state government's website. Another way to find this information is by searching for it using a search engine such as Google. Use the words "colleges", "universities", and the name of your province or state as search criteria. See? I told you a computer would be an indispensable tool!

In the mean time, here is a list of questions that will help you determine if distance education is something that would work for you. Give each question some serious thought and then answer the questions honestly.

- Is feeling that you are part of a class important to you? Remember that this is something that you will not be able to experience with distance education.

- Would you consider yourself someone who prefers to get things done ahead of time, or do you either procrastinate or fail to complete them? If you have trouble staying on task and managing your time, you may have difficulty keeping focused on your studies, and may fall behind.

- Are classroom discussions important to you? Again, you will not have classroom time with other students.

- When a teacher hands out instructions, do you prefer to figure them out on your own, or do you ask questions seeking clarification?

- Do you need commentary on your marked assignments immediately, or do you feel comfortable waiting a few weeks?

- Consider your current daily schedule. Do you feel that you will have ample time to take a course in a traditional classroom setting?

- How easy or difficult is it for you to attend classes on a regular basis?

- Do you consider yourself to be a below average, average or above average reader? If your reading comprehension is weak, studying alone and trying to make sense of the materials may be more difficult for you.

Once you've considered the questions and given yourself honest answers, you'll have a better idea if distance education will be a suitable option for you and your lifestyle. You'll need a high level of motivation and self-discipline. Although this type of learning is certainly not for everyone, if you are the type of person who can be committed you'll have no problem succeeding. Most institutions will suggest that you dedicate 15 to 20 hours to school work per week and that falls pretty much in line with the time you'd need to pursue studies in a traditional classroom setting as well. Also, if you increase the number of courses you take at a time, the amount of hours you will need will increase as well.

I can comfortably work full-time, raise my children, keep some family time set aside and take two courses. I have also taken three at a time, and I do not recommend it, nor will I ever do it again (just my two cents). Although you may think, "Well, what's one more?" the additional time you need to spend on a third course when added to normal everyday life can become the straw that broke the camel's back. My life went from manageable to unmanageable, and all of my courses suffered for it, not to mention my family and home life. I had less time to devote to each course, resulting in lower grades and way more frustration than I needed. I also had significantly less time for my family. My downtime – the time that everyone needs to just relax, was drastically reduced as well, creating a cranky, stressed-out mom.

While you're pondering those questions, here is one more. How easy will it be for your family to accommodate your new schedule? My husband and children all had to take on additional roles and responsibilities as attending classes required me to be away from the house two nights per week, as well as needing additional time to read, study and write essays. Occasionally I also had to take time out on the weekends to meet up with classmates to work on group projects and presentations. All of these hours add up!

So to help you out, let's look at a regular week in my life. If you work full-time and have kids, your life will probably resemble mine a great deal once you take on the added job of going to school.

Monday

5:30 a.m.	Get up, shower, get ready for work, make lunches
7:30 a.m.	Leave for work

8:00 a.m. – 4 p.m.	Work (read at lunch)
4:20 p.m.	Hit grocery store for supper items
4:40 p.m.	Pick up daughter at day care
5:00 p.m.	Get home and start supper, spend some time with husband and kids
6:30 – 7:00 p.m.	Start on homework, assignments or reading
9:00 p.m.	Bed time for daughter
9:15 – 10:00 p.m.	Read some more
10:00 p.m.	Get ready for bed and hit the hay

Monday to Friday look pretty much the same with the exception of two nights per week, when I would leave work at 4:00 p.m., drive home, get changed, grab my books and laptop, make a sandwich to eat on the way, hit the road, drive 45 minutes to campus and make it to class by 6:00 p.m. I would leave school somewhere around 9:00 p.m., arriving home at about 10:00 p.m. Remember that this was taking two classes per semester. If you add that third class in there, all hell breaks loose!

The weekends consist of trying to squeeze 2 or 3 hours of reading in on both Saturday and Sunday, unless I have something that is coming due for a class, at which point it would be quite normal for mom to be locked away for most of the day while everyone else tried to keep up with housework and went along with their lives.

Does this sound crazy? It is, but it's temporary, and worth it in the end. But what does this craziness mean to the rest of the family? We'll talk about that in the next chapter.

If you do not have children, this will be much simpler. Trying to make sure that you have time set aside to be a parent (which should be the number one job anyway) can sometimes be a struggle. If you are kidless, that stress doesn't exist.

If you are single, then more power to you. You definitely won't have the guilt factor of being away so much included in your daily life. Accommodating an education into your daily schedule will be much easier.

By using distance education, you can avoid being away for hours on end, but you are still responsible for completing the work as assigned and reading all the material. These tasks take up a lot of time, and I have found that the reading lists for distance courses seem to be heavier than classes on campus. I think they do this to make up for the time that you're not traveling. Perhaps it's some evil plan on their part to make you pay for the privilege of plunking your butt down on a nice soft chair and reading while you enjoy a nice steaming hot cup of coffee while the others are sitting in hard, uncomfortable chairs and braving the elements. Cruel? Perhaps, but there's pros and cons in every situation, right?

For now, take some time to decide if you're prepared to spend the next few years living with this kind of schedule. It's tiring but the rewards are plentiful.

Four

Everyone Into the Pool!

*I am always willing to learn,
however I do not always like to be taught.*
~Winston Churchill

I applied to university when my daughter was one. I had decided to start classes but I don't think that either my husband or I had really thought things through very well. I remember the image of my baby girl hoisted up in her daddy's arms waving bye-bye to mommy. By the time I got home, she'd be in bed sleeping and I would have missed the entire evening with her.

What I soon figured out was that I just simply couldn't keep up with my reading with a young baby in the house and everything was beginning to suffer. I was missing out on a lot of her "firsts" and it was breaking my heart. After about a month of this, I decided to withdraw from the courses and was lucky to get about 80% of my money back. I knew without a doubt that I would return to school, but that it would have to wait until she was older. I don't regret that decision at all. Timing is everything.

I loved being in class and loved the interaction with adults even more. Having my mind stimulated again was like a dream. I was participating in discussions and learning new things. But was that worth what I was giving up? Not for a minute.

My husband was nowhere near prepared for what my absence would mean to him either. He was forced to take on a much bigger role than he ever had in the past. My son was just turning eleven, and the baby was one. Neither of us realized the magnitude of changes that we'd have to make in our lives. Now, we knew better for the next time.

If you're single, you can just skip this entire chapter. Go on. Git. You don't need to read this. You're welcome to stay and read on if you really want to, but none of it will apply. Just giving you a little friendly warning.

Where was I. Oh yes. Getting prepared. Communication is the key, people. You need to talk to your partner and make some plans. Who's going to pick up the kids? Can alternate arrangements be made? What if Monday Night Bowling and Thursday's Movie Night have to be cancelled? Who can get home to let the dogs out? Can you afford the added cost of school? Will your workplace allow you to modify your hours if needed? Do one of you work shift work? Will there always be someone home for the kids? Can you both agree to plan vacations around school?

These are all things that need to be addressed, sooner rather than later. Talk to your partner and figure out what the issues are that pertain to you as a family as one of you goes back to school.

If you've got children, bring them into the discussion as well when you see fit. If you have older children, as I did when I finally went back, what added responsibilities can they take on to help out? In my case, my son took on the role of babysitter until dad got home. Some days this also included him making them both something to eat. The kitchen didn't always get cleaned up, but I could deal with that. In fact I'm not nearly as uptight now about a messy house than I was before school! This also meant that he gave up two nights of after school activities and came home to look after his sister. Was it fair to ask him to do that? Maybe, maybe not. But he was old enough, and was happy to help out. There were of course times when we made alternate arrangements so that he wouldn't miss out on the more important things. After all, it wasn't his idea for me to go back to school.

Simple household chores had to be realigned as well. Instead of leaving the laundry piled up on the floor waiting for mom to do it, everyone pitched in and did a load. Dad even learned how to grocery shop. He still isn't the wisest shopper in the world, but at least there was food in the house.

If school is going to be a burden financially, you'll have to work out the budget and decide what is going to work and what isn't. It may be that some things will need to be sacrificed for a while if needed. Can you all exist with 20 channels instead of 500? Does someone really need the $200 shoes, or will $50 shoes be acceptable? These topics may be unpopular in your house, but it's better to make the decisions beforehand rather than waiting and busting out the nasty surprises later on your unsuspecting family. Resentment at having to give things up to accommodate your education may not be very pleasant.

Will you need to take out a loan? What are your options regarding payment? Will your partner need to take on a second job?

If you are planning on going full-time, you may qualify for a student loan. These loans may not require payment until after your education is complete. If your partner makes too much money though, it is possible that your loan application will be denied.

Look on the school websites for grant and bursary opportunities. These are non-repayable sums of money. You will need to apply for them but it could be worth the time it takes to fill out the forms. Wouldn't it be nice to receive one of them every year to help pay for your tuition and books? Some workplaces also have grants available to employees who attend school on a part-time basis while employed. It may be worthwhile asking if yours offers anything.

Try to think of all the possible questions and situations that could arise and at the very least have some frank discussions about them. They may come into play or they may not, but at least you will have had the opportunity to contemplate them before they pop up.

Discuss your reasons for going back to school with your children. Be honest with them. If a better job will be the result, let them know that. If more money will be the result, let them know that too. Explain that you're making sacrifices for the good of the family. Kids understand and will appreciate your openness.

My eight year old daughter understands the reasons. She counts down the days until I'm done, wishing that mom could stay home and do things with her. She knows that it's not forever and that my reasons for doing it are to improve our lives.

My son has benefited from my experience as well. Now that he has spent all these years watching me struggle with work and school, he has no desire to do things the way I did. He understands that attending university now, instead of waiting until he has financial obligations and a family of his own is a much better idea.

Anything is possible with a little forethought and some planning. This should be an enjoyable experience for you, and it can be more enjoyable with a well thought out plan in place to back you up.

Five

Applying to a School

It is important that students bring a certain ragamuffin, barefoot, irreverence to their studies; they are not here to worship what is known, but to question it.
~ Jacob Chanowski

Once you've made the decision to go to school, you've decided either on attending classes or pursuing the distance education route, had discussions with your family and picked the school or schools you'd like to apply to, it's time break out the forms and get started.

Here in Ontario, applications for the majority of colleges and universities must be submitted to the Ontario Universities' Application Centre, or the Ontario College Application Service. Once these bodies receive your application and applicable fees, they will forward your application to the relevant institutions. Not all schools subscribe to this service. Some institutions prefer that you apply directly to them. To determine whether the school you wish to apply to requires you to use a service or apply to them directly, visit their website to find the information you need. This information will usually be listed under the Registrar's Office.

The United States has a very similar service. To find the

service you need, simply use a search engine like Google, and use words such as "university", "college", "application" and the name of your state. The application services also have websites, and usually contain lists of colleges and universities that subscribe to their service. Keep in mind that you will likely have to pay a fee per application. So for example if you apply to only one school, the fee may be $100. However, if you apply to five, the fee can be $500.

You will also have to get official transcripts from any other post-secondary institution you have attended as well as the high school you graduated from. Photocopies are not acceptable. There is a nominal fee to request a transcript from colleges and universities, however high schools will generally give you one free of charge.

The subscription services offer all of the information you will need to apply on their website, including lists, requirements, costs, forms and practically anything else you can think of. If there are entrance tests you must take they may also have a section focusing on those. If you are required to write an essay to go along with your application (which is generally only required in the States) the website may also offer hints and advice on writing them. In all, these websites are a virtual cornucopia of information. Take advantage of them, and spend some time poking around.

If the school you want to apply to does not use these services, you will be able to find all the necessary information listed on their websites, including the required forms. Whichever route you take, make sure that you review what you have filled in and check it for spelling errors, omissions, and correct information. You'd feel terrible if you were waiting for a reply only to find out that you'd provided them with the wrong mailing address!

If you have some previous education from another institution, you may qualify for transfer credits. The school will use the transcripts you supply them with to determine whether you qualify for any. This is only applicable to education received at a college or other university. When I applied to Brock, I had spent 2 years at a community college studying Graphic Arts Electronic Pre-Press. I was awarded 2.5 transfer credits from Brock for my previous education. These credits meant that instead of starting with zero credits, I now had 2.5 in my favour, which was better than nothing! These credits covered all of my elective requirements.

Remember those majors and minors we talked about earlier? When you fill out your application, you will have the choice of applying to a particular program, or applying with an undeclared major. If you enroll with an undeclared major, you can follow the course selections for the program you're interested in without making a declaration right away. At some point in your studies, you will be asked to declare a major.

Once you've taken a few courses, you may decide that you'd prefer to pursue a different major and you are free to switch at any time. If you have already declared a major, you can change at any time simply by filling out the required forms. There may or may not be a fee associated with this.

Do you remember the two terms I promised to explain? One was a required course and the other was a letter of permission.

A required course is a course that you are required to take for your particular major. For example, with my combined degree, there were two French and one English courses that I was obligated to take before I could register for higher level courses. The other course choices were up to my discretion as long as they were part of my program. All programs will have required courses. If you try to register for a course before taking a required course or a pre-requisite course, you will be unable to register.

A pre-requisite course is simply a course that must be completed with a passing grade before you are allowed to register for certain other courses. For example, the first-year French grammar course is a pre-requisite to any of the second-year grammar courses.

A letter of permission is a letter granting you permission to take courses at another institution, usually issued by the dean of the faculty. Most schools will require that you have taken and successfully completed a certain number of courses before you will be allowed to take a class at another school. You're welcome to take whatever course you wish to, wherever you like, however if you don't have a letter of permission, the course will not count towards your degree. The course must also be relevant to your program and the material similar to one offered at your home school. Brock University requires that you have five Brock credits under your belt before they will permit you to do this. Transfer credits don't count either. They must be credits from your home institution. Again, rules around this subject may vary from school to school. It is wise to investigate all the rules before registering in a course at another institution. Otherwise you may end up spending $800 on a course that cannot be used towards your degree. That's a huge waste of money, time and effort.

If you were unsuccessful in gaining admission to the institution you chose, take a look at the reasons why. Don't be afraid to call the school and ask. It may be simply be that you need to take some upgrading courses. Ask the school where you were denied what you can do to secure admission in the future.

Eventually, you will receive a letter in the mail either welcoming you to the school or advising you that you were unsuccessful. If you've been accepted, you will receive a student number included in your package. This number will allow you to go online and register for classes. You must have your student number to do this. If you have any questions or problems, contact the Registrar's Office and they will point you in the right direction. You may also have to visit the school to get your student card and have your picture taken.

One person you should get to know right away is an academic advisor. This is a person whose role it is to help you figure out what path you need to follow and which courses you need to take. Even if you have not declared a major, you can still make an appointment with an advisor. These people will make sure that you stay on the right track.

I recommend that you visit an advisor at least once a year prior to picking new classes for the upcoming semesters, especially if your degree is going to take longer than the normal 3 or 4 years. My degree will take a total of five years to complete, and every summer I make an appointment with my advisor to review my course selections. There are instances where program requirements change, so it's a good idea to keep in touch with this person to make sure that you're taking the right courses all the way through.

In my case, having a combined degree, I actually had two advisors - one responsible for the English department and one for the French department. Even though there were two, I opted to use only the English department advisor. She was able to access the information from the French department as well, and was more than capable of giving me advice for both. These appointments are well worth your time. You can usually find the name of these advisors on the Registrar's Office page.

Six

Not the Kitchen Table

A mind once stretched by a new idea
never regains its original dimensions.
- Anonymous

With suppertime fast approaching I looked at the kitchen table one day and thought, "We can't eat here. I can't even see the table." The table, or what was once the kitchen table, was covered with piles of books, papers, laptop, dictionary, journal articles, pens, two empty coffee cups, one still half full, and a plate of crumbs.

I moved into the dining room to survey that area. Not great, but better. Newspapers, another dictionary, more journal articles, two more dictionaries, a few pens scattered around, my reading glasses, some crumpled up paper, a textbook and my notebook containing my scribbled notes for the outline of my most current essay.

I was quickly discovering that this was not such a great scenario. My schoolwork was taking over the house, like some ever-growing plant. You know the kind that starts off as something very pretty and small, and everyone says, "Oh, how beautiful!" Then before you know it, the damn thing has increased exponentially in size, like some steroid-pumping junkie and taken over the entire yard, and threatens to move briskly into your neighbors' yard.

Well, that's what my mess was turning into. I knew I had to get a handle on it before my family was forced to move out. But what to do? That was the question. I needed a 'place'.

I had tried setting up shop when needed on our bed, but every time I got comfortable my eyes got heavy and I wanted to sleep. That wasn't going to work either.

Schoolwork takes up space. There's no doubt about it. Your personal library will increase in size, and some of the books you'll have to buy are monsters themselves with huge price tags attached. Some years my book collection grew by eight or nine books per semester!

I started looking around the house, making a plan. We have three bedrooms on the main floor, and one big bedroom downstairs that was being used as a storage room of sorts. My cousin had lived with us for a few years while she attended McMaster University and this room had served as her bedroom. When she left, she left a lot of her stuff in this room. At this point, she was in Australia attending teacher's college. A plan started to come together.

If I moved my son's bedroom down to this room, and moved some of Kristin's furniture upstairs to my son's vacated bedroom, I could piece together a den of sorts. A place for me and my stuff. My own little room where I could shut the door and work in peace. It sounded like heaven.

I enlisted everyone's help immediately, laid out the plan, and we all set to work. I think they were secretly ecstatic that I would have a room dedicated to my stuff, and they wouldn't be tripping over it anymore. No one complained about having to help either!

We moved in a desk and chair, and ran an Ethernet cable up through the floor so that I could be online. We brought in an old tv stand and tv, and filled up the lower shelves with my books. We moved an old couch in, and I bought a nice slipcover for it as well as a few throw pillows. Next I rescued both my husband's and my college diplomas and hung them on the wall. A lamp and coffee table were next, and voila, the room was done.

Rules were made. This was my room where I could read, study and write my essays in peace and quiet without being disturbed. When the door was closed, it was closed for a reason. It was a good plan.

As a side note, one of our family dogs, a 90-pound retired greyhound named Trap, took over the couch and claimed it as his own. It's not often that he's not walking along behind me (he's my shadow), but on the rare occasion that I managed to get into the den without him knowing and closed the door, he would stand in the hall whining and crying to be let in. Lesson learned? Make sure Trap is in the room and asleep on the couch before attempting to get any work done.

I highly suggest that you find a suitable space in your home where you can get away and do what you need to do. Having leftovers from dinner stuck to the paper you need to hand in tomorrow is frustrating and not really acceptable. If you can work in a more orderly fashion and have all your resource materials nearby you're setting yourself up for success, not to mention a neater house. Having a place where you can get away from the usual house noise is ideal. It can be difficult to stay focused while kids are running in and out of the house or the phone is ringing. Being able to see the pile of dirty dishes on the kitchen counter is counter-productive. If you're like me, you'll have an uncontrollable urge to get up and clean them. If you're tucked safely away from the "house" you can concentrate on "school" and leave the "house" for later.

If you don't have a spare room, a corner in your bedroom or living room where you can set up a small desk and perhaps have a bookshelf would work nicely, and allow you to have a workspace. Having a dedicated place to sit down and work uninterrupted allows you to work more efficiently and more effectively.

There are a few very important items you'll need to arm yourself with. I have found that when I didn't have these things close at hand it drove me nuts. I spent more time getting up and walking to get them than actually working.

First, are dictionaries. You really need to have a good quality dictionary, and I'm not talking about those little pocket versions either. I'm talking about the great big suckers. They cost upwards of about $80, but are worth every single penny. If you are studying languages, like literature or another language altogether dictionaries in each language as well as an English/other language dictionary are a good thing to have. I have four of these big ones - one in English, one in French, one French/English, and one that encompasses literary terms. They were a bit of an expense, but I'm so glad I bought them. My children use them as well and will for years to come.

A decent printer is another great tool and can be purchased at reasonable prices from stores that carry computer equipment as well as other big box stores, and smaller specialty stores. If you can afford the up front higher cost of a laser printer, it will actually save you money in the long run. Print cartridges for deskjet or inkjet models don't last very long and are outrageously expensive to replace. I've actually purchased an entirely new printer for less money than replacing the ink cartridges for the old one would have been. Laser toner cartridges are more money, but last significantly longer and are more cost effective. You will be printing a fair bit, including your essays, anything you're researching online, journal articles, assignments, etc, so having a printer is almost a necessity.

A bookshelf is one of those things that aren't necessary, but really nice to have. Otherwise, you end up with piles of books on the floor, effectively redecorating your room with furniture made out of books.

I had mentioned that we filled up the bottom shelves of the tv stand with books. It worked for a little while, until each shelf was stacked two deep. Then as more books were purchased, they ended up being stacked beside the tv stand on the floor. Next, they started moving out into the hallway as if they had a life of their own. It was time to invest in a piece of furniture to house them.

I love books. I can't get rid of them. I'm sure it's some sort of sickness. Once a book arrives in my house, it's there to stay, living out its life in a loving environment. This problem of mine encompasses reference books, novels, cookbooks, textbooks, literature books, anthologies, hard covers, paperbacks, e-books that have been printed off, how-to books. This list goes on. Online bookstores and I are tight. Real tight.

Next on the list of important things is a stapler. Seriously. Professors hate it when you hand in ten or twelve pages, and it's not stapled together. You also run the risk of pages getting separated and lost, which has actually happened to me. It's frustrating for both the student and the person reading and marking your work.

I had a 2-part assignment to hand in. I had stapled one part together, but had forgotten to staple the other part together in my haste to get to school on time. I folded the corners down hoping that they would stay together. They didn't. When my assignment was returned to me, my mark was very low, and only half was returned - the stapled half. I questioned the professor about it, and he swore that he didn't have the other half. I learned my lesson.

Having said all of this, if you can't swing the room or the furniture, a comfortable spot on the couch will work, or even the kitchen or dining room table. Don't feel that you MUST have all of these things in order to become a successful student. They are nice, and create a more comfortable and orderly working environment, but they are not necessary. (Except the stapler. Definitely buy a stapler.) A printer however, is a necessity. If you're going to attend classes on campus, there may be a computer commons area where you'll be able to print off what you need. This service usually has a nominal fee of a few cents per page, to cover the cost of the paper. If there is such a place on campus at your school there will likely be computers there as well that are free for you to use.

When it comes time to study for exams, you will really need a quiet place. If you can commandeer a room in your house to use, it will make studying much easier. Interruptions are the biggest problem, more so than noise. There have been times when I've packed my bag and headed out of the house in order to get away from all the distractions to study. I have studied quite effectively in a coffee shop at a little table in the corner. There was noise and people milling about, but none of it was directed right at me and so I was able to tune it all out and focus. I also use my office at work a lot in the evenings and on weekends if I really need absolute peace and quiet. (Note: more time away from home) My fish Maurice, who lives in my office is always happy to see me and grateful for the company.

When you are writing essays or studying. Take frequent breaks; at least one 10-15 minute break per hour. Get up, walk around, stretch, get a drink or a piece of fruit or other healthy snack. This will keep you from getting really stiff and tired, and the snack will help make sure your energy level stays up. Do not start studying or writing your essay the day before it's due. It's generally a bad idea. As adults with busy lives, it's quite normal for "life" things to pop up at the last minute and at the most inopportune times. Sick children, meetings, unexpected guests, family and medical emergencies - any number of things can happen when you've planned on spending that time working on your studies. It makes much more sense to have it done beforehand just in case something unforeseen arises.

Seven

Time Management

*Give me six hours to chop down a tree
and I will spend the first four sharpening the axe.*
~ Abraham Lincoln

Old Abe was really onto something here. As I spoke briefly about in the last chapter, careful planning and good time management can really cut down on the amount of work you need to do as well as the length time you're going to need to do it. I am famous for sitting down to write an essay with absolutely no plan. Does it work? Not really. I waste more time than anything. I know what I should be doing. I come from a long line of teachers who have drilled it into to my head, but still I usually refuse to listen and suffer the consequences.

I'm not going to tell you what I do. Instead I'm going to tell you what I should be doing, and what I now preach to my children. You know that old saying – Do as I say, not as I do. This is one of those times when it's really applicable.

Try to set a time aside everyday that you devote to school, even if all you can find is an hour. This would be in addition to the hours you'll be spending on campus if you're attending classes. If you're going the route of distance education, you'll probably need more than an hour per day, but it's up to your discretion. On the weekends try to find a three or four stretch. You can break that up into smaller periods of time, but I wouldn't plan on any less than three hours. You can use this time to read, review your notes from class or prepare assignments. It's a good idea to read the material for the following class once without taking any notes, then reread it, this time jotting down notes and/or questions. You will be responsible for having the material read before class and to arrive in class prepared.

Writing essays will require time over and above the time you've allotted for your day-to-day work and will require time to prepare your outline and do your research as well.

As an example, I'll use a topic that was given to me in one of my French classes (although it was in French when it was given to me).

Explain the use and function of setting
in French-Canadian literature.

As soon as you receive the topics for your essay, start thinking about them. Choose one as soon as possible, and start to develop a plan and put it on paper. Include passages that you found interesting or applicable to the topic. Jot down themes you noticed in your readings. Create a point-form list of points you want to make.

Essays are more or less divided into three parts, although it can be a little more complex than that, and each needs to be carefully planned, researched and crafted. There are different types of essay, but you'll learn about these in your first year of school. The introduction contains your thesis, or what you are going to argue. The body contains all the facts and information, the "meat" of your argument, and the conclusion is the part where you say, "There, that's how I proved my argument".

First of all, you need to define what your thesis is. Yes, the topic is setting in French-Canadian literature, but you need to decide what aspect of that you are going to argue. Next, you need to decide what your arguments are, outline and explain them, and prove them using references and your own words. Once you've done that, you need to conclude, explaining how and why your arguments validate your thesis.

Once you've got all that sorted out, you need to actually find the references you are going to use. Universities and colleges will almost always have a library. Most will also have a link to the library on their website where you can look for books, and perform online searches for journals articles and such. This type of search can be done from your computer at home. You will need to become very familiar with this, and learn how to get the most out of your searches. You'll be doing a lot of searching. There are usually librarians who can help you out if you are unsure how to perform a search or just generally lost with the whole library experience. Once you have got your references, you're ready to go. The material you've researched will need to be included in your essay, however be very careful to avoid plagiarism. If you plagiarize, you'll be awarded a big, fat zero for your efforts as well as having some disciplinary action taken against you.

I mentioned before that you should start as soon as possible. As you become proficient in the art of essay writing you'll be better able to gauge how much time you'll need to spend preparing and working on it. In the beginning, give yourself as much time as possible. Set aside a few hours every weekend to work on it, and if possible, allot some time in the evenings during the week. Set a date that you expect to be finished and try to make sure that it's at least a week before the essay is due. Remember that you will need time to proofread your essay and make revisions.

As a rule of thumb, I kept one night per week free where no books were opened. Generally this was a Friday night and I wouldn't open a book, nor would I even spend one moment thinking about school. This was a night for me and my family to either do something together, or to just relax at home. It's important to ensure that you've got time set aside to do nothing. If you don't keep enough free time for yourself, it's easy to get bogged down and fed up. I've seen people give up their studies because they felt overwhelmed and unhappy. By ensuring that you make your free time as important as school time, there will be less of a chance that this will happen to you.

So what happens when you want to take a vacation? Do you plan only to take holidays during summers and spring break? You certainly don't need to, and to be quite honest, you couldn't pay me to take a week off to travel somewhere hot during spring break.

I have traveled with my family during school, but I make sure that I read everything that I would have read had I been in class. You can also ask classmates to share their notes with you from the classes you missed. Most students are happy to do this, and will ask you to return the favour sometime. Missing one class is fine as long as you're comfortable with the material you are studying. If you feel that missing a class is going to be detrimental, then I would postpone the vacation for a little while. Use your own judgment when deciding when to take a vacation. You are the only person who will know if it's going to affect your studies negatively or whether you will be able to catch up. Speak with your professor as well, and let him or her know that you will be away that week. I have never had a problem moving due dates or arranging to write tests a week earlier than everyone else.

So let's say that you've booked the vacation and you're packing your bags. Do you bring schoolbooks with you? Generally, if we're on vacation I opt to leave everything associated with school at home. It's supposed to be a vacation, and time spent with your partner and family; not school on a beach or the ski hill. Having said that, I think there were two times when I did bring a book with me, but it was because I was truly enjoying the book. Remember that I studied English literature so most of the things I was reading were stories, not calculus or biology.

Don't be afraid to allow yourself some downtime. Everyone needs to have time to relax and unwind. Besides, those margueritas will be more enjoyable with good conversation rather than with a textbook. When you return home to work and your studies you'll feel refreshed and ready to dive back in.

Eight

Can I be of Service?

The important thing is not to stop questioning.
~ Albert Einstein

If you look around enough, you'll discover that colleges and universities have a lot more to offer than just classes. There are people who can help you learn how to write an essay and people who will walk you to your car at night after class if you are nervous about walking to the parking lot in the dark. There are some great resources in schools ripe for the picking. You just need to take the time to find them.

Orientation sessions are widely available and generally run in the summer months. You can attend one of these sessions to figure out where you are on campus, where you need to go and how to get there. They will answer your questions and help you transition into life as a student. They will likely be able to provide you with information about the services available on campus as well.

If your school has a gym, you should be eligible for a free membership entitling you to use all the equipment at no cost. This may include the pool if they have one. If you are within driving distance you can take advantage of all these things. There are sports to play, teams to join and sweat to be sweated!

Some institutions also offer learning skills services where you can sharpen existing learning strategies and develop new ones as well. They can help you to build confidence and get the needed motivation to be successful with the increased demands of post-secondary education. Help in becoming a better reader and help with your writing skills may also be offered. You can find tutors to help you get through the spots you may be struggling with too. These services may be available in different formats, such as one on one, a drop-in basis or group meetings.

Some schools also offer personal counseling services if there are things in your life you need help with or just need someone to talk to.

If you've got the freedom and the financial ability to do so, there are also study and work abroad opportunities. Some institutions have affiliations with schools in other countries, and offer a semester or full academic year of classes abroad. There are costs involved with this, but it's truly a wonderful opportunity. Some schools will even contribute some money to help you along!

Childcare is often available as well. When I went to college, my son was only 4, and if you remember, I was alone in a new city. Daycare for him was weighing heavily on my mind. Upon visiting the school, I discovered the day care services and arranged for him to attend. It was perfect! He came with me in the morning and stayed all day. Lunch and snacks were provided. They took part in some early learning activities like number and letter recognition, did arts and crafts, had reading time, nap time, and generally had a ton of fun everyday. He was so sad when he "graduated" and was no longer attending.

Institutions also offer services for students with disabilities. Whether it be physical, medical, sensory or a learning disorder, an education is still available to you with their help to ease the road. Everyone is entitled to an education.

Co-op services are usually also available, allowing you to integrate your academic studies with relevant work experience. This may be only available to full-time students however.

By spending time browsing every nook and cranny of your school's website, you'll probably be surprised by the amount of services they offer and by the variety of things available to you as a student. By participating in them, your educational experience will be enriched and I promise you'll meet many new and interesting people. So take some time to get familiarized with your new school. Get involved and take part!

Nine

Ten Steps to Success

Most successful men have not achieved their distinction by having some new talent or opportunity presented to them. They have developed the opportunity that was at hand.
~ Bruce Barton

Being a successful student is more than just getting good grades. It's enjoying your time in school, and truly benefiting from your time there by taking part in what's available and being an active participant in your classes. It's having the ability to balance your life and juggle your responsibilities effectively. If you are stressed and overwhelmed, you probably won't enjoy your education and you'll get much less out of it. You've got something the students coming directly out of high school don't have. Life experience. Put it to work for you by setting goals and recognizing priorities.

Be involved in your classes and feel free to participate. If you are actively engaged in your class, you'll be more likely to retain the information.

So let's review a little bit and look at ten steps that will help ensure your success.

1. Organize your finances and prepare a budget before you enroll in school. Have frank discussions with your partner about the realities of school life and how they will affect your family.

2. Organize your time. Plan sufficient time for studying, classes, exercise, sleeping and free time. Keep family time an important part of your everyday life.

3. Relax. Take time out for you. Read something other than a school book. Continue to participate in activities that you enjoy and make a point of doing things that will make you smile.

4. Set goals for yourself. Where do you want to be in four or five years? Can you realistically expect to have your education completed in that timeframe? Take a workshop to sharpen your learning skills.

5. Feel successful. Take advantage of the many job and volunteer opportunities available.

6. Go to your classes. Participate in discussions, seminars and study groups. Set up a study group with your peers. You can all help each other.

7. Enjoy your campus. Spend time on campus taking advantage of the services they offer. Make use of the facilities, and visit the library. Make new friends. You won't be the only mature student there.

8. Eat nutritious meals. Look after your health and stay fit, healthy and active.

9. Study. Have a good study plan; one that fits into your life. Work smart – not just hard. Review your work often to cut down on study time for tests. Take good notes.

10. Use the services. Use the services that have been designed to help students succeed. Seek out help when you need it. If you can't find it, ask.

Life is too short to put off the things that you really want to do. Even though you may have to wait a little if circumstances require it, follow through on your dreams. Enjoy yourself and put your time and money to good use. Feel good about what you achieve and don't expect that everything you do is going to be worthy of an A+. Do your best and you'll be satisfied. Lead by example and show your children the value of an education. But most importantly of all, have fun. Life should be full of smiles and no regrets.